Untitled

Haronepthia Cameron

First published by Haronepthia Cameron
ISBN 978-1-939761-38-5

Printed in the United States of America

Haronepthia Cameron
102 Lundy Lane
Jonesboro, GA 30238

www.voyagersolutions.net

Cover designed by Neon Alfred

Dedication

This book is dedicated to each person who is hurting and searching for love in all the wrong places.

There is a GREATER LOVE!

I dedicate this project to all the readers past, present, and future. May this be a useful tool to assist you on your voyage through life.

Acknowledgments

I acknowledge God, for He said He will direct my path if I will acknowledge Him in all of my ways. He is my Savior and my Counselor.

Thank you to my husband, Tommy Cameron, who has helped me with my journey in more ways than one.

I would like to acknowledge my mother, Emma Jean Sands, who gave me everything she had to give. I love and appreciate you, Mom.

I acknowledge my children, Terrence McLaurin and Jeremy McLaurin, who helped train me as we grew up together.

Thank you to my women's fellowship group, including Tracey Jones, Earnestine Nelson, and Tracey Powell, for their encouragement and meaningful feedback.

I thank my sister, Connie Judge Johnson, for her spiritual support and for challenging me through the birth of this project.

I also acknowledge Ashley for her feedback and diligence for meeting with me on a consistent basis to help launch this project, as well as my beta readers, Racine, Adrian, and Debra.

Contents

Introduction

My heart goes out to women of today. By the age of 12 or 13, girls have been through so much that molds their thought process about how to have a relationship. By the age of 20, many have suffered so much abuse that their self-worth is through the floor (notice I did not say through the roof). I say that because the behavior exhibited by many women is destructive. The things they do to be accepted, to be popular, and to get a boyfriend are often demeaning, demoralizing, and full of disappointment, leaving them with a sense of powerlessness. The pain from each breakup is so severe it sometimes causes them to act irrationally. Having started such guy-pleasing behavior at a young age without any guidance other than the mistakes and disappointments of the past often leads to a repeat of the same errors and a decrease in self-worth each time the cycle is repeated.

Here's an example of what I'm talking about. A young girl, 12 years old, likes looking at music videos with her friends. In the videos, she sees a pattern of girls dancing with very little clothing on and guys singing, calling girls bitches and whores. The girls in the videos are smiling and laughing. They look as though they are having a wonderful time. Often in the videos the guys move from one girl to the next. Each girl performs for his pleasure by doing whatever it takes to get his attention. Another scene often portrayed in videos and movies is the female back-biting. As girls turn on one another the guy sits back feeling good about himself because he has numerous girls fighting over him. The competition becomes so intense that normal reasoning is warped.

By the time a young lady turns 13, boys begin to notice her and she likes the attention. Oftentimes, she has received no guidance or healthy input about relationships and self-worth, and even if she has been taught by her parents, peer pressure often has the most influence. The only instruction she has had is what she has seen on TV, videos, movies, or witnessing verbally or physically unhealthy relationships played out in front of her eyes on a daily basis. So what does she do when she begins to get noticed by boys? She believes to keep his attention she must do whatever he wants her to do or he will move on to someone else. Whatever he tells her, she believes it, even though there are little alarms going off inside telling her not to do certain things.

Her need for love and acceptance pushes the override button. She stops listening to herself and instead looks to the guy to lead her and tell her what's right or wrong, good or bad. She loses her voice that God gave her. Rather than speak for herself, she waits for the guy's reaction to dictate her next move. Unfortunately, he does not stick around long, so she is hurt, disappointed, and left with the thought that maybe she should have done more to hold on to him. She enters the next relationship with this warped thinking, and the new guy recognizes her vulnerability. He senses that he can get whatever he wants from her and he uses it to his advantage until he moves on to another. Of course, he blames the girl for the breakup or fallout. He may say things such as, "You are too easy," "You're not a challenge," or "You're not pretty enough or sexy enough." Each time the cycle repeats itself she loses a little more of herself and the beautiful young woman God created her to be.

This way of thinking is embedded in her, and she carries it into adulthood, maybe with a little more discretion, but the cycle is the same. The discretion is the lie she tells herself to cover up the embarrassment and shame each time a relationship fails. By day, she looks like a confident, well-put-together woman, but by night she beats on a man's door uninvited, drives around looking for him, or calls his phone repeatedly even though it is clear he is ignoring her.

The more he ignores her the more desperate she becomes. Things she used to cover up out of shame begin to show up in her daily life. The feelings of rejection and desperation begin to push forth uncontrollably. Often the behavior used to attract men, such as wearing revealing clothes or performing sexual acts, may become part of her action plan to gain love and acceptance. She tries new things that cause a man to lust after her, but never to love her because he never gets to know the wonderful person she was created to be. He does not get to know the real woman (the original creation) because, in fact, she doesn't know who she is.

She has no clue who she is or how she got to this point in her life. She has reached a place where she acts out the same behavior in a different costume with different scenery and different characters. The one main character remains constant, and that's her. As the cycle continues, she adopts habits and behaviors to help suppress the disappointments, such as drinking, smoking, unprotected sex, using drugs, self-mutilation, and sometimes attempting suicide. In reality, these behaviors she hopes will bring relief, are self-destructive.

Your story may be different, but it is likely seeds were planted throughout your life that threaten the abundant life God promised you. Now is the time to confront those past experiences and to dig out the roots that have grown into fear, insecurity, uncertainty, and hopelessness. It's time to live the life of success you've always dreamed of. Being unaware of the issues that lurk beneath the surface can lead to a frustrated and unfulfilled life.

Success is not measured by people, things, or money, but rather by fulfillment of purpose and peace of mind. You might believe that if only you had money, a man, a house, or a car you would finally be happy. Although these are nice things to have, they will not fulfill your dreams until you address the root growing beneath the surface in your heart and innermost thoughts.

This book will introduce you to some of the roots that may be lurking beneath the surface of your life that prevent you from moving forward in your purpose and experiencing the abundant life that has been promised to you. This is an exciting journey in which you are the voyager. Use this book as a journal to track your journey and learn things about yourself.

What you write down is to help you become aware, not to cause you to judge. Answering the questions with short answers is like cutting off the top of a tree without removing the roots. It is crucial to apply yourself and allow the roots to be exposed so they can be replaced with things that are pure, noble, and praiseworthy. Approach this journey with determination, commitment, and purpose.

Chapter 1
Steps to Discovering Your Roots

Many things fueled my development as a young person. I started out with a very close relationship with my father, and I knew I was the apple of his eye. Every day when he came home from work I insisted on sitting on his knee to eat with him. It seemed as if the food just tasted better because it came from his plate. I wasn't hungry for food, but I was hungry for Daddy's attention, and I needed it replenished every day. I looked forward to it. I was Daddy's little girl, and I believed I was more special than anyone else in our home. If there were money problems or marital problems, I had no clue. I was in my own world, which is what little girls should experience with their fathers. The introduction of alcohol in my family soon changed this, which eventually stalled my emotional development and led to my emotional needs going unattended.

I believe the relationship between parents and children is critical to self-identity and self-respect. These primary relationships are where children get the first messages on how they should be treated or loved. That is the way God intended it to be. Parents are to be a demonstration of God's love to their daughters and sons. Unfortunately, in our society that is not always the case. The quality time children need with their parents is sometimes disrupted by single-parent households, child abuse, spousal abuse, and financial deficiencies.

Humans are born with the need to feel loved, accepted, and valued. When this need is unmet, children learn to survive without it. Survival, however, is not the same as success. Despite being able to function without the emotional foundation necessary to live a fulfilling life, those needs still exist, often buried deep inside. The needs do not go away.

As children grow into adults with unmet emotional needs they often seek fulfillment in ways that may not bring forth the best outcomes. Being unfulfilled can leave an adult with strong desires to be accepted and loved. These desires can lead a person to do things they would not normally do, such as being in an abusive relationship in which they are not respected. The decisions they make trying to obtain love are nothing less than sacrificial. Seeking love from a place of unfulfilled emotional desires can lead to a repeated cycle of going in and out of relationships or staying in a relationship that shows very little respect, not truly satisfying either party. Many habits may be formed during this survival mode, such as drinking, using drugs, over working, or not working at all, and can lead to emotional conditions, such as depression. Very often, this leads the unfulfilled woman into a state of desperation for the love she seeks, but never seems to find.

The Desperate Desire for Love
Desperation is usually not recognized by the person, but others can see it. Many women have become so adept at covering up this desperation that they wholeheartedly deny it.

One woman I counseled could not understand why her relationships didn't last. She was in a relationship where she constantly tested her boyfriend by inquiring of his where-abouts, and then not believing his explanations. She would act in ways she knew were irritating just to see if he loved her enough to tolerate her behavior. Of course, she saw nothing wrong with these desperate patterns; she just felt that if he loved her enough he would be patient with her. When her boyfriend became frustrated, the relationship ended. She lamented that she had given so much of her-self in the relationship with her efforts being unappreciated or not returned. She carried her feelings of rejection from one relationship to another, repeating the cycle. Through our sessions, we identified her fear of rejection and her constant need for reassurance of love and value. She was going about it the wrong way.

Another young lady, beautiful, smart, and full of potential, was involved with a young man who was formerly incarcer-ated, unemployed, and dealing drugs. On occasion, he phys-ically abused her, and she eventually became pregnant. After her parents refused to allow her to live at home with her boyfriend, she found herself with no place to live, involved in a dead-end relationship. Although she had offers for lodging, she refused the assistance because she felt loyal to him and said if he couldn't come neither would she. I asked the ques-tion, "Why stay with someone who abuses and disrespects you when you are so beautiful and smart, and pregnant?" The answer she gave was that she loved him. There was no self-love, but she exhibited a desperate need to fulfill something inside she hadn't yet identified. She did not see her despera-tion for love and acceptance, nor what that desperation was leading her to become and how it clouded her ability to make sensible decisions.

When your relationships do not look the way you think they should you should take a look and see what may be at the root of your decision to stay in that relationship. If you choose to do the work, are bold enough to take this voyage, allow yourself to be healed, and are willing to make decisions based on something other than past hurts, fears, or what you may have missed out on, I invite you to continue.

Honor the Voice Within

Understanding the root of your decision-making is critical as you journey through life. Each of us has a voice within that directs our decisions. Journaling is one of the best ways to identify what motivates you, determine the root of your behavior, and discover how to overcome the challenges you face. Journaling allows you to be honest because no one will judge you or tell you what you should feel; you can just write your feelings honestly.

As you journal, be careful not to judge yourself. Avoid statements such as "I should," or "I know right from wrong," "I know better than that," or even condemning statements such as "I am so stupid to be putting up with him, this, or that." When you honor your voice through journaling, simply begin your statements by saying "I am . . ." or "I feel . . ."

For example, a woman in an unhappy relationship may journal something like this: "I am so tired of giving, giving, giving in this relationship. He makes me sick. I don't know why he won't treat me right. I always give him support and I am there for him whenever he needs me, but he is never there for me. He does not appreciate all the things I do for him.

I make sacrifices for him. I'll stay up late if he needs me to and I listen if he needs to talk. I helped him when he was going through school and starting a new job. I carried the load when he had nothing. He doesn't even love me enough to plan a simple date for us now and then. He has the nerve to cheat with another woman while I am here sacrificing myself. Why do I keep attracting the same type of man? Why do I keep putting up with this kind of treatment?"

Journaling something like this is a good start. Next you should answer the questions you asked. Why do you continue in the destructive cycle? Find the root of the decision you have made to continue the same way expecting him to change.

Your conversation may be a little different, but this is one example of how to begin your journaling experience.

As you write, don't concern yourself with proper grammar and punctuation. This is freedom time. The only criteria are to be honest with yourself and to hurt no one else.

Please, please take this time to set the foundation for your voyage!

Now that we have reviewed the proper use of this tool called journaling, let's move forward. Tell the truth about your life without being judged or fearful of being rejected. Pay attention to how you feel and give voice to those feelings. You cannot embrace or change what you will not acknowledge. As you give attention to your voice, change can take place. The small voice takes you to the root of the matter.

Unveiling Your True Emotions

Listening to your feelings without apologizing for them is vital to your voyage. If something bothers you, admit it. If you don't, the first person you lie to is yourself. If you have feelings of low self-worth, loneliness, frustration, or fear of rejection, but you don't acknowledge them, they will unknowingly impact your decisions. These ignored emotions, feelings, and thought patterns will make a place for themselves without your awareness. The unfortunate thing about such feelings is that they have been looked upon as negative; therefore there is the tendency to hide them. Hiding or ignoring your true emotions is the beginning stage of silencing the voice within. If you are feeling anger, pain, disappointment, rejection, depression, or frustration, write about it in your journal. You may write something like, "I get so mad at him for not giving me the attention I need ..."

Writing down such emotions helps you realize how you truly feel. You cannot overcome what you will not face. If you internalize these feelings you may become angry, bitter, and take them out on others, or just suppress them and make yourself sick. Either way you drive away the love God intended for you when He created you. So you learn not to listen to yourself and not to value yourself. Eventually, these emotions will be reflected back to you within your relationships. Because you are unaware that you have ignored and dishonored the feelings you have, you don't recognize yourself in the mirror of your partner's behavior. You only see what he is doing to you that is so wrong.

When you suppress your emotions you deny a very important part of your makeup. Emotions were given to us by God. Unfortunately, feelings often get a bad reputation. Emotions alone are not bad, but when they are out of control, ignored, or suppressed, they can cause negative outcomes. Your emotions may reveal the root cause of why you do the things you do, why you choose the wrong guy, why you put yourself in unhealthy situations, why you may make risky decisions, and why you are always making the sacrifices. When you sacrifice who you are to be who someone else wants you to be, the fruit of your relationship will never bring you peace, love, or happiness.

Do not get bogged down with what you think you ought to feel or overwhelmed with what others say about you, especially if they have a negative impact on you. From past experiences and bad advice, you may hear things such as, "Don't let it bother you that he is seeing somebody else; just try harder to please him." Sometimes others offer advice they think will make you tough; for example, "Don't let him see you cry," or "Don't let him know it bothers you."

What you're feeling is not about him, it's about you. This is not about putting on a front for anyone. It's time to listen to your heart and give yourself the attention you may really desire to come from someone else. Buried emotions can also mean buried dreams and ideas.

Facing the Truth

Once you have listened to the voice within and unveiled your true emotions, whether frustration, anger, or fear of being rejected, you must unpack the baggage. Begin to take responsibility for yourself. First, realize that if you are doing all the giving and very little receiving in your relationships there is a selfish motive behind your actions. Ask yourself why you are giving away so much attention to others and giving very little attention to yourself. When you feel as though you have nothing else to give, where does the energy come from to give a little bit more, to tolerate a little more of the unhealthy behavior that leads to a decrease in self-worth and increased emptiness?

Do you rationalize your behavior in any of these ways?
- "If I do this then he will appreciate me and treat me special. He will want to be with me. He won't cheat on me. He'll stay with me. He will marry me."
- "If I can just do the right thing to make people happy, they will not reject me."
- "If I can come up with the right action just to feel loved, appreciated, worthy, I will be worth keeping around."

Do you agree now that there are some selfish motives behind your actions? Your actions are often motivated by your desire to be accepted, loved, and valued. What's wrong with that? you may wonder. There is nothing wrong with love and appreciation; the problem is the manipulation that takes place to get it.

God gave you the very gift that you need; His ultimate love and acceptance. You must learn to walk in what has been given to you. "Seek ye first the kingdom of God and His righteousness and all these things shall be added unto you." You must be able to hear the voice God has given you to lead and guide you. You are created in the image of God. You must respect His creation—YOU. It is time to pay attention to you. Relationships are meant to empower, uplift, encourage, and promote. That's what should have happened in childhood. If it didn't, you can spend a lifetime trying to get it any way you can. Often, the message that starts very early in life is, "If I can just do the right thing or act the right way I will be loved, accepted, and appreciated." You received messages from various people during your developing years that have an impact on your current years.

This is your journey and you are worth every word you journal, every tear you cry, and every moment you give to yourself. Though you may face what appear to be negative emotions and messages, no root is so deep that it cannot be dug out and replaced with something beautiful. What will you plant in your garden of life? It's important to plant your own roses instead of always smelling somebody else's and expecting your life to change. What you think, say, and feel is important, so start digging. Here's your chance to be honest. The truth will set you free!

Begin by writing about your childhood.
When I was growing up my house/home was

What is/was your relationship with your mother like?
My mother and I are/were

What is/was your relationship with your father like?
My father and I are/were

_____

_____

_____

_____

_____

_____

_____

_____

_____

_____

_____

_____

_____

_____

Did you feel loved, secure, important, and cared for?
When I grew up I felt

_____

_____

_____

_____

_____

_____

Untitled

What were some of the words you remember being said about you or to you?

I remember hearing my mother/father/auntie/grand-mother/friends/peers say I

**What painful memories do you have from your childhood?
It hurt when**

Did you witness events or behaviors that made you feel angry or helpless?

I felt angry/helpless when

_____

_____

_____

_____

_____

_____

_____

_____

_____

_____

How do you feel now? What emotions are you feeling now that you have journaled about your early life?

Now I feel

_____

_____

_____

_____

_____

Do you feel love for yourself? If yes, how do you know?

Begin this by stating: I know I love myself because ... Or
you may write, I don't love myself because ... Or, I have been
working hard to get someone else to love me and ...

_____

_____

_____

_____

_____

_____

_____

_____

_____

_____

_____

_____

_____

_____

_____

_____

_____

**Nourish your roots as you dig deeper with this
Food For Thought:**

In the book of Matthew 6:30-34 in the Message translation of the Bible it reads:

"If God gives such attention to the appearance of wildflowers—most of which are never even seen—don't you think He'll attend to you, take pride in you, do His best for you? What I'm trying to do here is to get you to relax, to not be so preoccupied with getting, so you can respond to God's giving. People who don't know God and the way He works fuss over these things, but you know both God and how He works. Steep your life in God-reality, God-initiative, God-provisions. Don't worry about missing out. You'll find all your everyday human concerns will be met. Give your entire attention to what God is doing right now, and don't get worked up about what may or may not happen tomorrow. God will help you deal with whatever hard things come up when the time comes."

Trust and believe you are loved and are very important to God, and cherish the beauty of who you are.

Chapter 2

The Cycles of Failure

As life unfolds, painful experiences from failed relationships can be implanted into your emotional tank that may cause you to become emotionally numb. Some seeds of failure may have been planted in your life over which you had no control, and others you may have been aware of and chose to ignore. Some examples of these seeds may include neglect, rejection, physical abuse, harsh words, and sexual abuse. Regardless of how they may have originated, you have the power to overcome these obstacles.

Ecclesiastes 3:1-2 (Amplified version) states, "To everything there is a season, and a time for every matter *or* purpose under heaven. A time to be born and a time to die, a time to plant and a time to pluck up what is planted. . ." Therefore, all events have a limited time of actively producing results, whether wanted or unwanted. As time goes on, you must allow the painful parts of those experiences to die. Then you must pluck them up and plant new seeds to grow a harvest that produces a life that is fulfilling and healthy.

Begin to look for the treasure waiting to be discovered in you. Writing about your early relationships in the previous chapter should have opened up some doors to your emotional needs. Now is the time to take a look at how these experiences may be playing out in your life.

The Common Denominator

The cycle of failure works its influence in both intimate and less personal relationships. The key is to know who God says you are, apart from anything else, including your relationships with others. Consider the history of relationships you have been in or are currently unhappy in.

I have counseled with many young ladies who have come to me brokenhearted without a clue as to why they keep repeating the same cycle of failed relationships. I listen as they describe the relationship, then I ask what went wrong. Time and again these ladies tell me they gave all their love and worked so hard at the relationship, yet it was unappreciated in the end. Normally they tell me the guy did not respect them or started out wanting to be in a relationship then suddenly started acting like he didn't value them anymore.

I usually hear the words, "He hurt me," and "I'm so mad at him." Eventually, the relationship ends and the woman is left to either get over it, run after the guy, tolerate the disrespect, or try to figure out what happened. For many women, this happens over and over in their lives. If this scenario sounds familiar to you, remember that YOU are always present in your relationships; therefore, YOU are the common denominator. This does not make you the "bad person;" it just brings attention to what and whom you need to focus on.

Repeating the Fear Cycle

Painful events often produce fear; fear of that thing ever happening again. Fear then becomes the root from which future decisions are made. Here's an example.

A young lady was hurt in a relationship by a guy who was unfaithful. As a result, she became fearful of the same thing happening again. A new opportunity for a relationship was presented and immediately she decided to do specific things to keep the new guy from cheating on her. She set in motion behavior she believed would prevent him from cheating. At the very foundation of this potential relationship was fear, which produced the fruit of insecurity and people-pleasing, and became fertile ground for failure. This was the beginning of a sacrificial relationship or the end of a potentially good one before it really got started.

First of all, what's wrong with this picture? Where was her focus? It appears her focus was on controlling the behavior of her boyfriend. What was she spending her time and energy on? Her time was spent trying to figure out how not to get hurt or cheated on. No time was spent on whether or not this was an uplifting, encouraging, respectable person who would add to her life, not take away from it. She needed to know she could not control another person's behavior. If she put on a mask and became a puppet in order to please him she would not be respected.

You can only control what you do. When you focus on what you fear rather than what you need you will produce a harvest out of that fear. Fear will cause you to try so hard to get the other person to love you, give you attention, and treat you with respect that the relationship is really ignored and unfulfilling. Meanwhile, he will have to continuously prove he is not cheating. The work goes on and on. If the man isn't cheating he will soon move on because he will tire of the constant tactics to control him. The very thing you fear will show up because all your energy and time is spent on that which you fear. When you choose to love yourself, take care of yourself, and honor yourself, you will select a man who will do the same. You will attract what you reflect.

What you do to yourself is what you will accept from others. If you are loving, kind, and respectful to yourself you will tolerate nothing less from anyone else. Instead of trying to prevent someone from cheating on you, first stop cheating on yourself by trying to get someone else to love you more than you love yourself. If you do not take the time to do this for yourself you will repeat the cycle of broken relationships created by fear and insecurity. Fear can rule all your decisions. When you make decisions out of fear the results are usually destructive and sacrificial.

The Preemie Cycle
Giving yourself too soon in a relationship is what I call the Preemie Cycle. It is vital that you find out who you are and what you want before getting into a relationship. If you are lacking emotional fulfillment in your life, whether from childhood or more recent experiences with rejection, you will go into your next relationship looking for someone to fill that gap in your life. If your identity has not been established prior to the relationship, consciously or subconsciously, it will be built on trying to get someone else to define who you are. When a guy comes along and says all the things you want to hear this often feeds your hungry, unfulfilled emotions. As a result you may prematurely decide to yield to a person you don't even know, causing you to take chances that

may not be safe. If you are honest, there are times you know you shouldn't do things or you know something is not right, but it feels good to your hungry, unfulfilled emotions which speak louder than the instinct of protection God gave you.

Then the lies begin where you tell yourself he is different, he is good because he attends church, he treats me well, or at least he has a job. Unfortunately, your emotions silence the voice of God who wants the best for you. You ignore the warning signals inside that are there to protect you. Think of it like a traffic signal. The red light inside warns you that regardless of how sweet he talks or how nice he acts, do not proceed. STOP NOW!

The yellow light says proceed with caution; see him in social settings with friends that are discerning and smart and who operate in a healthy lifestyle. Take your time to see what he is really about. Continue to learn what you want and work on who you want to be, not who he wants you to be.

Even with a green light you must know who you are and fulfill your emotional well-being apart from the other person so you don't become needy and lose sight of who you are. When you don't allow the person God created you to be to develop and mature, you will repeat the Preemie Cycle, continuously entering into relationships prematurely. You repeat the cycle because you don't take the time to get to the root of who you are and experience the love God has for you.

Now that you see how the Preemie Cycle repeats itself, look a little deeper to find a way to change the fruit manifesting in your life. If you haven't noticed, the one thing that has remained constant in these examples is you. If you don't do the work of maturing in a love that is unconditional and consistent you will always need someone else to fulfill your needs. You are the common denominator. You can take responsibility for yourself. God gave you the power to change your life.

Journey a Little Deeper

Let's voyage into deeper waters. When you love you give of yourself endlessly. You're patient with your loved one, you make sacrifices for that person, you are faithful to that person, and you wouldn't dare betray them.

Have you done any of these things for yourself? If not, why not?

_____

_____

_____

_____

_____

_____

_____

Have you been patient with yourself, or have you been very demanding of yourself?

Why do you treat yourself the way you do?

———————————————
———————————————
———————————————
———————————————

Have you been thinking you should know the answers, you should know how to deal with these things, and you should be able to keep going? Have you been beating up on yourself, thinking you should be strong enough to walk away from this relationship or stay in this relationship, whichever it may be?

———————————————
———————————————
———————————————
———————————————
———————————————
———————————————
———————————————
———————————————
———————————————
———————————————
———————————————

What tools are you using to gain wisdom and direction?

How much time do you spend learning about the human brain (how your thoughts affect your actions), emotions, and spiritual part of your being?

You are a complex creation of God, and you must get to know the great person you are.

Take a minute and breathe. Now this next question is vital.

How many times have you cheated on or betrayed yourself?

_____

_____

_____

_____

_____

You may wonder how you could cheat on or betray yourself. Cheating on yourself might sound impossible, but whenever you continuously sacrifice yourself to try to obtain love and acceptance from others you are betraying yourself. When you get into relationships with others who don't honor and respect you, or when you give yourself to someone who thinks very little of you, you betray yourself before the other person even has a chance to do so.

Stop cheating on yourself and realize that God loves you regardless of any faults or shortcomings you may have. Visualize yourself in the sea of peace, with the warm arms of God wrapped around you in the form of the bright sunshine. Lie back in your sea of peace and vulnerability with your Father. Aren't you glad our Father God said He would never leave you or forsake you?

Although you are on a voyage you sometimes have to take a moment and float. Allow the warm waters of thought on this matter to embrace you while you recognize all the pressure you have placed on yourself. It's okay to shed a warm tear down your face from the fatigue of holding yourself up. Embrace the moment of just being who you are. Allow your higher being, God Almighty, to remove the load, and float in the melody of His arms.

During this time you may feel you want someone else to hold you. Resist going outside of yourself to get this. Embrace this opportunity to grow and set some emotions free. If you feel like crying, be patient with yourself and tell yourself it's okay to cry. The key is to give yourself what you want from another person. Give to yourself what you would give to him if he was feeling what you are feeling right now. Be as good and patient with yourself as you would be with someone else, and know that God loves you so much.

If you feel empty and alone you might feel as if you need or want more than God's love. There was a time when I felt this way. I eventually discovered that I was handling God the same way I was handling my other relationships. I was fearful of fully trusting and believing that He would do what I heard others talk about. Because I didn't really trust God, I needed Him to prove Himself to me. I had conditions in order for me to trust Him. This, of course, is a no-win situation.

After much pain and frustration, I went back to God without all the conditions, and decided to try to trust Him like I've never trusted anyone before. I began to talk to Him from my heart, and I admitted I didn't know how to trust Him. I was afraid to trust Him because I couldn't see Him. So many people had let me down that I found it hard to believe God wouldn't let me down too. I wanted my life to change. I asked God to show me how to trust and to show me what real love looks like. I began to read the Psalms and to listen to ministers who taught on the love of God. This helped me mature in a very different love. I must say I have no regrets. God changed my life forever. If He did it for me, I know He will do it for you. Romans 8:32 (King James Version) states, "He that spared not His own Son, but delivered him up for us all, how shall He not with him also freely give us all things?"

You can make Him Lord in your life as well by praying this prayer: "Heavenly Father, I come to You in the Name of Jesus. Acts 2:21 (New International Version) says 'And everyone who calls on the name of the Lord shall be saved.' I am calling on You, Lord, and I pray and ask You to come into my heart and be Lord over my life according to Romans 10:9-10 (King James Version): 'If thou shalt confess with thy mouth the Lord Jesus and shalt believe in thine heart that God has raised him from the dead, thou shalt be saved. For with the heart man believeth unto righteousness; and with the mouth confession is made unto salvation.' I confess that Jesus is Lord, and I believe in my heart that God raised Him from the dead. As Gloria Copeland always says; 'Lord take my life and do something with it.'"

The Process Continues
This process of getting to the root is not the easiest in the world, because you may not be accustomed to paying attention to yourself emotionally, listening to your feelings without judging yourself, or apologizing for what you feel. As

you journal, take the time to identify the emotions attached to what you are experiencing. If you don't face it you can't change it.

Discovering the driving force behind your decision-making is important. You have the power to remove any motivation that is unhealthy, but you must identify it. Pay attention to what you are thinking and feeling. Be honest with yourself rather than manipulating your life with emotional distractions, such as unhealthy relationships or habits.

Listen to that very small voice telling you that you are lovable, special, and worth the time and effort you put forth on your journey. In the beginning the voice may be hard to hear. As you give power to the voice you will hear it much better, and change can take place. The small voice leads you to the root of the matter. Once you understand where your emotions find rest you can apply the power of change to produce something different. You can do this through your journaling.

There will be many people and activities that will try to distract you from this process of journaling. Do not become discouraged or distracted. These things will probably sound more enticing than journaling does; they may even sound more important. Do not place your healing on hold. By putting youself on hold you may really be saying, "These things are more important than I am."

Don't do the same things and expect different results. Do not ignore the part of you that needs your undivided attention.

Do not betray or abandon the most precious gift God has given you: the wonderful creation of you. Make your voyage the priority for a change.

Take the time to think, meditate, pray, and journal your answers to these questions.

My destiny is

_____

_____

_____

_____

_____

_____

_____

_____

_____

_____

_____

_____

My short-term goals are:

1. _____

2. _____

3. _____

My desire is to

In order to do this I need

I believe God's purpose for my life is

What am I allowing to take priority over my process, what am I willing to do about it, and how?

Untitled

_____

_____

_____

_____

_____

_____

_____

_____

_____

_____

In the midst of this healing and journaling process your situation might begin to look as if it is improving. You might assume that the other person has finally changed or that you are completely healed from past issues. Regardless of what things seem to be, please continue this process. Most likely, as soon as you get comfortable with an even flow of life, many of those old issues will show up again, causing you to be even more frustrated and angry than before. Consequently, you might find yourself right back where you started, maybe a little more frustrated, and even angrier with the other individual because you feel as though they tricked you. It's a good time to be honest with you. Who are you really angry with? Who is responsible for your journey? Though this may be a difficult time to journal, it's important you do so.

The person I'm most angry with is

_____

_____

_____

_____

_____

_____

_____

_____

_____

_____

_____

_____

_____

_____

_____

_____

_____

_____

_____

_____

_____

_____

_____

_____

The reason I'm angry with this person is

_____

_____

_____

_____

_____

_____

_____

_____

_____

_____

The person responsible for my journey is

I am almost willing to bet you are angry with yourself because you allowed it to happen again. That's a lot of pride to swallow in order to admit that. It's okay. You are safe with your non-judgmental journal. You are not alone. This is your time to learn how to love yourself, not how to get someone else to love you.

Looking in the Mirror

Being ignored by the other individual in your relationship is a manifestation of the way you might be ignoring yourself. People often reflect back to you what you feel about yourself. Beneath the pep talks, false sense of pride, and inability to face what is hidden within the shell you have carefully built around yourself over the years is the real you. It is time to look in the mirror to see yourself for who you really are: a child of God.

Trying to stay happy or upbeat so your partner will like you is a tactic used to avoid pain and rejection. When you put on the mask and try to be what the other person wants instead of being yourself you avoid the fact that this may not be the person who should be in your life right now. What's at the root will produce the fruit you see manifesting in your life.

Breathe. Remember there is no one to fight. You are in a safe place. To admit this to yourself does not mean failure or that you are a bad person. This is only a bridge to healing. Like many people, you were probably taught at an early age that it's good to be liked. You may have tried to be the teacher's pet or the student to erase the chalk board, to be selected to the cheerleading squad or hired or promoted at work. The goal in life became being liked or approved. There is nothing wrong with being liked, but when being liked determines your worth, that's a problem!

What message are you sending out that's being reflected back to you in the mirror of your relationships? Is it hidden insecurity, anger, desperation, or an identity crisis?

A little motivation to look in the mirror.
Food For Thought:

If you are not willing to deal with you, why would you expect someone else to do so?

Galatians 6:4-5 (The Message): "Make a careful exploration of who you are and the work you have been given, and then sink yourself into that. Don't be impressed with yourself. Don't compare yourself with others. Each of you must take responsibility for doing the creative best you can with your own life."

Chapter 3

The Trap of the Blame Game

There is a definite difference between blaming yourself (or anyone else) for your situation and taking responsibility for it. Blame carries a feeling of condemnation and criticism without a positive outcome. When you take responsibility you own the failures and shortcomings as well as commit to the process of changing things for the better.

The goal for this part of the journey is to take what you have learned thus far about cycles of failure and look at them from the perspective of the role you play in the condition of your life. It is vital to your healing that you recognize how having an unknown root can manifest chaos in your life. In the previous chapter, fear was discussed. Now take a look at another root in action: blame.

You are moving into the arena of taking responsibility for yourself. It is important to pay attention to what you do and why you do it. Nothing grows or stays without being nourished in some way. So in your conflicts you must explore what you are nourishing. In other words, what are you getting out of the situation? Consider this example.

There was a lady who spent a great deal of time arguing with her husband. She would call him stupid, suggest that he was a terrible father to their children, as her father was to her. She would express that she hated sharing her space with him, but she never left. Her reason for remaining in the relationship was that she believed he wouldn't be able to care for himself or their children without her.

A deeper exploration of the issue revealed several problems. The first was that all her focus was on him and his shortcomings. Second, she failed to recognize the root of the situation and what was being nourished in order to keep the relationship going. Third, she had chosen a man with attributes similar to her father, whom she did not respect. If you notice, most of her complaints were about his ability to father his children. Again, things are usually not what they appear to be. On the surface, it just looked as if she had an awful husband who didn't do anything for his children. He clearly must provide her with something, or she really would leave.

Identifying the Root

According to the woman, her husband was of no benefit to his family, which is the same view she had of her father, who left her family when she was a little girl. Having been abandoned by her father, she carried the pain of rejection throughout her life, which turned into anger and bitterness. Her husband is the stand-in for her missing father. He provides her with the opportunity every day to tell her father what she thinks of him. The words she speaks to her husband every day are the words she really wants to say to her father, but he isn't available so she relieves her feelings on her hubby. She punishes him for not doing the things she feels her father should have done. She gets to hate her father and point out his faults on a daily basis, yet keep him close, which prevents her from feeling abandoned.

Her husband doesn't actually need her there to survive. In fact, she needs him as a focus of her anger. But leaving him would make her just like her father, whom she hates. This keeps her in the same position she was in as a child: angry, fearful, and resentful toward the man in her life. As an adult, however, she gets to speak her mind. As long as her husband is available she will never have to forgive her father. She can stay tied up in hubby and all the stuff he is not taking care of so she will never have to look in the mirror and take responsibility for her feelings of unforgiveness toward her father. She will never experience the life of love because the roots of anger and unforgiveness continuously nourish the situation to produce the type of fruit that keeps her frustrated and unhappy.

Unforgiveness is at the root of this situation, and bitterness fuels the fire that controls this relationship. The deep desire to be loved and taken care of keeps her angry because she never seems to receive it. She must deal with what's underneath, at the root, rather than focusing on what she sees on the surface. The healing begins when she acknowledges her pain and anger. She must realize who she is really angry with, and make a conscious decision to forgive her father and begin to build an identity apart from that of an abandoned child.

Opening up suppressed childhood emotions is difficult, but necessary. If you find any familiarity with this story that reveals areas where you might be harboring unforgiveness, you must find the strength to release it. Learn to love yourself and allow yourself to weep, mourn your loss, or be angry with the person who hurt you, and not with the stand-in person. Forgiveness is necessary in order to realize who you are and eventually move into the love, healing, and acceptance of yourself. By avoiding the root, you will continue to create an unhealthy environment until you deal with the cause, and then change your way of thinking, believing, and behaving. You were created by God to be loved and appreciated, and He has given you the ability to forgive the most painful events.

Unforgiveness

Unforgiveness lies at the base of a lot of unsuccessful relationships. Unforgiveness can affect how you think and make decisions that impact your life. I heard someone give this description of "as a man thinketh so is he." You can have in your possession a beautiful water hose, of an original design, even made of gold. You take that water hose and hook it up to a sewer line and nasty stuff will come out. It is amazing how people dress up the outside with beautiful, sometimes expensive, clothing, jewelry, hair, nails, etc., but give no time to what lies on the inside, at the core of their being.

If unforgiveness and bitterness are at the core they will ooze out, like the sewage through the beautiful water hose. Often, unforgiveness will lie dormant for a period of time in your heart. Denial might step in and convince you that everything is good, that you're not angry, or that you don't care anymore. Eventually, the unforgiveness on the inside will come out, usually when you least expect it. Believe me, it's normally pretty stinky.

If you believe someone else is responsible for your happiness or unhappiness and they don't do what you think they should to show their love or appreciation for you, then more than likely you are angry. Unforgiveness breeds anger, and the more you do for the other person, the angrier you become because you are not receiving what you think you deserve in return. Anger and unforgiveness typically walk hand in hand, and they increase in intensity with your acts of what you call love. Often, however, these acts of love are manipulation tactics designed to convince someone to love you. You have to ask yourself, "Is my motivation love or is it trying to manipulate someone into loving me?"

Not dealing with the anger and unforgiveness in one relationship often leads to the very same pattern in future relationships. You may be able to attract relationships, but are unable to keep one. No matter how you try to pretend you are okay on the outside the fruit of unforgiveness will manifest itself. This will often drive people away because with unforgiveness, anger, and hurt comes the need to avoid being hurt again. This can lead to subtle manipulation and controlling behavior sugar-coated with kindness and so-called love. The sad part is that most of the time you won't recognize it. In your mind you will be the victim because you believe you are giving, loving, and kind, and that your partner doesn't love you as much as you love him. This creates more unforgiveness, and the cycle continues.

Unforgiveness may be the root in this situation, but there may be other roots that impact your relationships. Many times, the hurt has only been pushed to the side or put on the back burner and temporarily forgotten. Forgetting about it does not mean the issues have been dealt with. You can create circumstances that provide distractions so you will not have to deal with your feelings. Until you give unforgiveness the attention it requires to conquer it, it will always have permission to cause chaos. Don't expect success until you clean up the mess.

Look in the mirror and find the root you may be nourishing. Trying to cut it off by ignoring your pain and unhealthy thoughts will only cause it to grow back. Instead, make a commitment to dig it out so there is no possibility of reoccurrence, only success. It is almost impossible to move on completely until you experience forgiveness of yourself and of others. Now is a good time to examine your roots because therein lies your lifeline and the quality of fruit you will produce.

Examine your relationships and the part you play in them. Psalms 51 is a good scripture to pray as you seek truth in your inward parts. Write down whatever comes to mind, even if you think it's not important. You are worth the investment you are making each and every day. Keep your eyes on you. No one and nothing can stand in your way. You are becoming more powerful every day.

Roots that often influence me are . . . (love, fear , anger, bitterness, frustration, etc.)

Why?

_____

Addressing forgiveness is a daily practice that may not be easy at first. Do not give up. Acknowledge and recognize when you are practicing habits that are unhealthy, then seek positive ways to correct them.

You are not exposing your faults to judge yourself harshly or to beat yourself down. Remember, your purpose is to heal. Quiet any negative thoughts by saying, "I am not here to compare myself to anyone. I am here to learn how to listen to myself and to understand what real love is all about. Condemning myself is not an act of love." Do not allow condemnation to rule in your life!

Take Action By Recognizing the Storms in Your Life

When you are focused only on pleasing others you become a shell, a robot that continuously creates storms and chaos and then blames others for it. Like a tornado, this behavior is destructive, and it leaves you feeling like a powerless victim. For a tornado to occur, the conditions must be right. Think about the conditions caused by the lack of self-love in your life.

Review some of the feelings you have written about earlier. Can you read this and recognize a person who wants to be loved? I am not referring to the outside defensive shell that has developed and identified itself as the real you. I am referring to the one who has worked so hard to get approval, the one who feels she does not really deserve love and happiness since she hasn't received it thus for. Maybe it leaves you with a secret. There may be a hidden fear of being neglected or rejected. These secret fears can be damaging to your future.

Secrets often bring shame, which creates favorable conditions for storms to develop in your life. You may feel you must keep this covered up so you have to live a lie of hope and faith, when every day it becomes more and more difficult to get up and put on your face. The lie you live every day only makes you love yourself less, because you hate the life you are living. Therefore, you hate yourself and look for someone else to love you out of your mess.

Making choices out of the deep secrets can lead to choosing the wrong person, as well as tolerating or doing things you really don't like. Your relationships are unfulfilling, so you try harder to please your partner, or you quit the relationship altogether only to repeat the pattern with someone else. Either way the conditions of rejection, failure, and lack of love increase every time you go through the cycle. The small drops of rain (disappointments) in your life become a thunderstorm as time passes, and nothing has changed. Deep down inside, when you meet someone new, your unspoken hope is that they will prove you are wrong about yourself.

This neediness, fear, and anger lead to the tornado of another broken relationship. Momentarily you feel stripped. The only thing you know how to do is rebuild the shell. Nothing changes inside. You (yes, I said you) continue to create the little storms in your life that provide the favorable conditions for the tornado, which continuously creates destruction and chaos. Everything you work so hard to build is subject to destruction because your foundation is weak. It is built on someone else loving you instead of you loving yourself and knowing that God loves you above all. Under these conditions you cannot receive love because there is a part of you that repels it. You want love, but you don't believe it can really happen for you.

It is extremely important to love yourself. You must first know—not think, not have faith, but know—you are capable of being loved. The way you come to that realization is by taking the time to experience love first hand, given by the one and only you. How can you love God or even another person when you can't love the person you live with every day—you?

What's at the core of your beliefs about past relationships?

Are you a victim? If so, what makes you a victim?

Are you angry?

I am angry because

Who do you need to forgive so you can go on with your life?

I need to forgive _____ **for**

_____

_____

_____

_____

_____

_____

_____

_____

_____

_____

_____

_____

_____

_____

_____

_____

_____

_____

_____

_____

_____

What can you do to begin taking responsibility for your actions?

I am taking responsibility for

_____

_____

_____

_____

_____

_____

_____

_____

_____

_____

_____

_____

_____

_____

_____

_____

_____

_____

_____

Untitled

Nourish your roots as you dig deeper with this Food For Thought:

Is it possible that sometimes you may feel a little jealous of other people who are doing okay; a little angry at somebody who may be moving on without you, or dare you say, at God, since He is the one blessing them and not blessing you? It's okay; don't judge. Nobody's mad at you for feeling what you feel, not even God. Really, you may ask? The answer is no, not even God. You are not doing anything outside of God's ability to heal with His love. He encourages you to be honest with yourself and rid yourself of hidden roots of darkness.

Be filled with the light of God's love so darkness can no longer dwell in you and rule your life. You can lie to or ignore yourself for so long that the truth doesn't seem true anymore. Therefore, it is necessary to allow Him into the hidden areas that have not been dealt with. Tell the truth so the root (the beginning) of a wrong thought may be pulled up, never to produce that type of fruit again. Then replace it with the truth of God's love for you.

No longer are you focused on pleasing everyone else. Instead, you are focused on developing yourself and being all you were created to be. Give others the opportunity to meet you, the real you. Give yourself the chance to experience the real you as well.

Matthew 11: 28-30 (Amplified Version):
"Come to Me, all you who labor and are heavy-laden and overburdened, and I will cause you to rest. [I will ease and relieve and refresh your souls.]

Take My yoke upon you and learn of Me, for I am gentle (meek) and humble (lowly) in heart, and you will find rest (relief and ease and refreshment and recreation and blessed quiet) for your souls.

For My yoke is wholesome (useful, good—not harsh, hard, sharp, or pressing, but comfortable, gracious, and pleasant), and My burden is light and easy to be borne."

Chapter 4

You Are No Longer the Sacrifice

So far, you have examined a few roots that are usually the cause of many manifestations of unproductive fruit. Now, consider how you may have sacrificed yourself over and over again and called it something else. Sometimes this sacrifice is called humility, submission, conservativeness, turning the other cheek, patience, and yes, even love.

When you enter into a relationship with someone who disrespects you and fails to honor you as the wonderful person God created you to be, you become the sacrifice. You continue to sacrifice your ideas, ambitions, desires, dreams, and purpose in order to maintain that relationship. Whether it is on a job or in a personal or intimate relationship, you sacrifice a part of you every day out of fear of losing the relationship and being alone. You may fear speaking up for yourself because the other person does not approve. As a result, you try to please the other person and you sacrifice your own needs to stay in a relationship that is unhealthy. I have only named a few things here just to help you understand the sacrifice you may have made or may make in the future if you do not learn how to love yourself and accept the love God has for you.

Self-sacrifice will never be enough to satisfy you or anyone else. If you have begun a relationship from a standpoint of sacrifice, your partner may demand more sacrificing as time goes on. Your purpose becomes pleasing him, leaving very little room for your true purpose to be fulfilled. Please understand I am not putting the other person down, nor am I lifting him up. I am still focusing on you and your decision to be the sacrifice that can never fulfill or satisfy.

The sacrificial training begins early in life. Parents, teachers, and other role models sometimes unwittingly reward good behavior and punish anything that is considered "bad" behavior without explanation. The sacrificial performance often begins because there is a human need to be accepted and rewarded. The response of others is based on your performance. If you do well, behave yourself, get good grades, work hard, and otherwise perform appropriately, you receive the rewards of attention and praise. The challenge comes when the performance is used to determine your worth.

A performance-based life with no foundation of love is a life of sacrifice. Most often, you are left with an unfulfilled life of your own. Some of the symptoms of an unfulfilled life are depression, discouragement, loneliness (even in the presence of others), and fatigue. You may find yourself making a statement like this: "I'm always there for others, but nobody is there for me." This sacrifice is at the expense of your own health and well-being. The tired feeling can be debilitating and overwhelming. You can do good things, be there for others, and get the promotions and the relationships, but the price is high when it is all based on your performance and the sacrificing of your own needs.

Every human is born with a natural desire for love. Unconditional love is what you should strive for. Avoid situations where you find yourself sacrificing to get the approval of others. If you don't care enough about yourself to stop sacrificing to get the approval of others, you will always be tired, burdened, and downright depressed. The emotional roller coaster of being up one day and down the next few days will eventually cause you to burn out.

Time to Rebuild

Through the challenges of not always getting it right on the money, you learn just how much you really need God. How wonderful it is to have a Father who loves you so much, one who cares more about your learning the lesson than punishing you. He does not desire to take you down, but to raise you up in His love. So if you make a mistake, don't try to hide it. Be honest and look for the lesson which indeed leads to the blessing.

You have been journaling about all the things you need to release, to get rid of, and to clean out. Now you need to begin to build a firm foundation that will sustain you for the rest of your life. I am going to share some scenarios and scriptures with you that I suggest you hold on to and use on a daily basis to build your identity. They are not just words. Envision the Father saying them to you personally. Talk to Him and ask Him to show you what love looks like, feels like, and how to accept and live in His unconditional love.

Rewrite the scriptures below to make them personal to you, as well as search out your own scriptures to give a stable answer to whatever the need may be in your life. Find your identity in one who does not change with circumstances, moods, and emotions. Jesus is the same yesterday, today, and forever (Hebrews 13:8).

Identity (Who am I?)

2 Corinthians 5:17 (Amplified)
"Therefore, if anyone is in Christ, he is a new creation. The old has passed away; behold, the new has come."

Rewrite example: "I am in Christ and am a new creation. Old things (unhealthy relationships, abusive relationships, low self-esteem, etc.) have passed away and I have become new (healthy, whole, loved, respected, and precious). YEAH!

James 1:18 (New Living Translation)
"He chose to give birth to us by giving us His true word. And we, out of all creation, became His prized possession."

Rewrite and make it personal for you.

_____

_____

_____

_____

_____

_____

_____

_____

_____

_____

_____

_____

_____

_____

_____

_____

_____

John 15:15 (New King James)

"Henceforth, I call you not servants; for the servant knoweth not what his lord doeth: but I have called you friends; for all things that I have heard of my Father I have made known unto you."

Rewrite and make it personal for you.

Ephesians 1:11 (New Living Translation)
"Furthermore, because we are united with Christ, we have received an inheritance from God, for he chose us in advance, and he makes everything work out according to his plan."

Feeling Lonely (Your Promise)

Deuteronomy 31:6 (New International)
"Be strong and courageous. Do not be afraid or terrified because of them, for the Lord your God goes with you; he will **never** leave you nor **forsake** you."

How can you make this personal for you? Rewrite it as if God is talking directly to you.

Deuteronomy 31:8 (New International Version)
"The Lord himself goes before you and will be with you; he will never leave you nor forsake you. Do not be afraid; do not be discouraged."

Rewrite and make it personal for you.

Psalm 9:10 (New International Version)

"Those who know your name trust in you, for you, Lord, have never forsaken those who seek you."

Rewrite and make it personal for you.

Psalm 94:14 (New International Version)
"For the Lord will not reject his people; he will never forsake his inheritance."

Rewrite and make it personal for you.

_____

_____

_____

_____

_____

_____

_____

_____

_____

_____

_____

_____

_____

_____

_____

_____

_____

_____

Feeling Un-loved (Your Promise)

Psalm 52:8 (New International Version)
"But I am like an olive tree flourishing in the house of God;
I trust in God's unfailing love for ever and ever."

Rewrite and make it personal for you.

_____

_____

_____

_____

_____

_____

_____

_____

_____

_____

_____

_____

_____

_____

_____

Psalm 69:13 (New International Version)
"But I pray to you, Lord, in the time of your favor; in your great love, O God, answer me with your sure salvation."

Rewrite and make it personal for you.

_____

_____

_____

_____

_____

_____

_____

_____

_____

_____

_____

_____

_____

_____

_____

_____

_____

_____

_____

_____

_____

_____

_____

_____

_____

_____

_____

_____

_____

_____

_____

1 John 4:10 (New International Version)
"This is love: not that we loved God, but that He loved us and sent His Son as an atoning sacrifice for our sins."

Rewrite and make it personal for you.

_____

_____

_____

_____

_____

_____

_____

_____

_____

_____

_____

_____

_____

_____

_____

_____

_____

_____

_____

_____

_____

_____

_____

Find promises to go with each of your concerns and write them in your journal. You may have to remind yourself of your new foundation until it becomes a part of you.

Do not turn this into a performance; it is the beginning of a relationship!

These are the seeds that will develop the roots to produce the fruit of a more abundant life. The relationship with God is a relationship that **gives,** so receive what your Father has for you. It's not the time to be a good Christian or even a good person so you can feel good about yourself or so someone else will feel good about you. It's time to be naked before the Father and know that He looks at you and says, "My child, my hurting child, I love you so much, and I will show you the way."

New Love, and Yet the Oldest Ever

Sweet, sweet daughter, I wrap my arms around you in my mind and my heart. My desire is to reach out to you in the midst of the very depths of your pain and disappointments. I want you to know how beautiful, unique, and special you are. God wants you to know who He says you are. Not only are you unique, you are lovable and loved by me and by God. You may wonder how I could possibly love you without know-ing you. Well, the answer is, your God, the Father who cares enough to pay attention to your needs and address your pain through me, knows everything about you. He states in the Bible that you are fearfully and wonderfully made. That's not just a scripture or a way to be religious. I know for a fact that He really means it, and I want you to know it for a fact as well.

Though you have been through pain, rejection, and disappointments, they were events and not identifiers of who you are. Your experiences do not get to define who you are. If you want to know who you are, look in the mirror that reflects the wonderful being God created you to be. Stand firm on what your loving Father says you are. According to Psalm 139:14, you are fearfully and wonderfully made. Yes, you. These are not just words in a book that have no meaning. According to Deuteronomy 7:6, you are God's most prized possession. Psalm 17 describes you as the apple of His eye.

God's reflection of you in the mirror of His words describes you as powerful when you choose to believe Him. In Hebrews 13:5, He says to fear not for He is always with you and He will never forsake you. God sets the standard of love. Use the Bible as a guide to determine if it's love or lust. If it doesn't look like His love, don't sink your heart into it. Stop looking for Love in all the wrong places and measure it by God's love for you.

If only you knew just how special you are. There is no one like you. Once you understand what a masterpiece you are, no one can touch you in a demeaning, demoralizing way again. The Bible tells us in Hosea 4:6 that people perish due to lack of knowledge. If you don't know your worth you will always allow someone else to define you and assess your value. You are precious in the sight of God. You may wonder how I know that. Hold up the mirror of the Word of God. Hold it up and find yourself in it, the true self that is unmovable regardless of any negative words that may have been spoken to you in the past, any rejection you may have experienced, or any mistakes you have made. You see, your Father's love is unconditional. God loves you because of who He is, not because of who you are; therefore, His love is stable, permanent, and unchanging.

You, my daughter, were made from greatness. I don't care what it looks like to you currently, because circumstances are ever-changing, but God's declarations about you remain steadfast and unmovable. The only thing that moves is your thoughts and feelings. When you look in the mirror of your experiences of rejection and messages of not being enough, when you begin to believe the lies circumstances have told you, it's easy to lose your sense of being special. If you only look at what experiences and people have told you that you don't have, you will never know what you do have and what you have the ability to become.

I want you to know this love I discovered as I journeyed through my own life. I walked through a childhood with an alcoholic father who was one of the sweetest men you will ever know, but his love for his daughter (me) was unstable and fluctuated with every drink. So I learned not to trust, and I didn't know what it felt like to feel safe in a relationship. He never hit me physically, but the pain of believing he loved something (alcohol) more than me was a constant rejection. That worked its way through my life. I found myself looking subconsciously for someone to love me and to stay around long enough so I would know I was lovable.

This hunger for love and acceptance often led me to make decisions in relationships that were not good for my well-being, situations where I could have been raped, abused, or even killed. These circumstances often left me feeling even less lovable than before. I even considered suicide in the name of "no love" and in the name of "I'm just so tired." What I was tired of was looking for love, acceptance, and a definition of who I am from something outside myself. I was the little girl who had lost the voice to speak out louder than my circumstances, to state who I am and what is disrespectful to me. I lost the power to make the decision not to choose relationships that subtract from, rather than add to, my well-being.

The key is respect, acceptance, and love. I had to start with me loving, honoring, and respecting the person God created me to be. It didn't happen overnight, but it happened. I came to know God personally. He is always there for me, and He wants to be there for you too.

Stop sacrificing yourself and remember who you are!

Remember Who You Are
by Haronepthia Cameron

You are not
The violent words you hear or say
You are not
The cruelty brought to this day
You are not
The one that needs to fit in
You are not
The one that has to pretend
You are
The one created by divine hands
You are
The one who's strong and can take a stand
You are
The one who can truly make a difference
You are
The one who can manage life with temperance
You are
Special just because you were born
You may
At times feel tired, weary, and worn
You know
Life has many twists, turns, and crooks
You have
What it takes no matter how it looks
You have
The ability to do what's good and brings health
You can
Forget who you are and do things that bring death
You can
Live life in a way that brings only strife
Or
You can
Remember who you are and decide to bring forth life.

What will you do?

Chapter 5

I Just Want to Share With You

I had a dream this morning, and in that dream many things were happening. It was as if I was in a park and there were people all around doing what people do in parks: laughing, playing, and talking. At the end of the park there was a house, and there were people on the porch laughing and talking. Suddenly, the men on the porch began to argue, and then they began to shoot people all around the park. The people who were not shot were taken hostage. I was one of the hostages. I was so frightened and I asked God what to do. I felt so helpless and powerless. It felt as though they had all the power and all the say-so in what would happen to me from this point on.

I woke up and I asked God what the dream meant. What came to me was that you can be happy one minute, and very quickly your life can take a dramatic shift, taking you hostage and destroying all you desire. He showed me how lurking thoughts and feelings of guilt (the house at the end of the park) in your place of happiness can take over and hold you hostage. He showed me how things I have done in the past that I felt guilty about subconsciously were lurking, waiting for an opportunity to steal my life away. When things did not go right in my life, the thought of me being punished for my mistakes would creep into my mind. I usually didn't pay much attention to these subtle thoughts.

This particular morning, as I continued to inquire about the dream, God said, "My GRACE and MERCY are more powerful than any mistake you could ever make." I had heard this before, but this day was different. He went on to show me that being born again means the thoughts of living according to the flesh (guilt, poverty, unworthiness, punishment) have to change, and a new birth needs to takes place.

I know I have messed up in the past, and there is nothing I can do to cover the wrongs I have done; however, Jesus came and showed me how to remove the guilt by allowing what he did on the cross to wash me in forgiveness and love. He paid for it so I don't have to keep paying every day. I didn't understand that until I realized I was continuously trying to pay for my wrong without even knowing it.

In grace, love, and mercy, He says, "I know, sweet baby girl, that you have messed up and made mistakes, but now you don't have to worry about it anymore; I took care of it all. You are not the sacrifice in this relationship; I am. Now I give you a brand new birth certificate and bring you into my family of love, peace, and prosperity with a Father who loves you so much and wants the very best for you."

I am honored and humbled to know I have a new birth certificate and a new family (not that I don't love my earthly family, but this is different). I am now part of something great and powerful and loving and full of potential. I am spirit, and I now walk in the Spirit by looking at what Jesus did and who He says I now am. I have a new life and a new identity. I needed God to be more than a story in the Bible, or a great God that the preachers talked about. I needed a God who is real, who could love me when I cried tears and felt pain. I needed a real God. I needed someone to love me who I did not have to perform for.

Not until I burned out did I slow down long enough to get to know Him as one who cares about me more than anyone I have ever known. All your earthly relationships—mother, father, husband, or child—require something of you, but God provides His love even before you know Him. This transformation doesn't happen overnight; it's a continuous relationship of getting to know your Father. Now, I want the same for you. Will you join me?

Who told you that you had to work hard to be loved?

_____

_____

_____

_____

_____

_____

Untitled

Who introduced you to love? How?

Who gets the final say-so about what love is?

Who will you put in charge and why?

God has one requirement, and that is to acknowledge Him in all your ways, and He will direct your path. Know that your life is in God's hands. You can turn to Him for guidance because He cares about everything that's going on in your life, even the little things. He does not judge you by your performance. He loves you through each and every lesson, each and every tear, and each and every challenge you experience. Learn to accept His love knowing He is not waiting to criticize you. He will never tell you you need to be different from who you truly are so He can love you. God created you, and He placed within you a gift. You are to appreciate and honor the gift He gave you. Allow God to use that gift to fulfill the purpose of your life.

As you love the gift of yourself, the passion of God will flow from you and bring to you what you have always desired. Simply accept God's love, and believe Him when He says He gave His only begotten Son so you can receive forgiveness of sins and a relationship with Him forever.

God's love is unconditional. Remind yourself of this often. Don't just get up in the morning and pray, say a scripture or meditate, and then put God down and continue your day. God is with you always, every minute of the day. He is real. He's right there loving on you, waiting for you to acknowledge Him throughout your day so He can direct your path.

God's love is not like any love you have ever experienced in your life, so it may take some getting used to. It may require constant reminding at first that He has His loving arms wrapped all around you every day, loving you, picking you up when you fall, encouraging you when you feel there is no hope, reminding you that you are His child when you feel you have messed up so bad no one could possibly think anything good about you.

Acknowledging Him allows you to be receptive to what your Father has for you. God loves you, and so do I.

What does it feel like to know you are loved uncondition-ally?

_____

_____

_____

_____

_____

_____

_____

_____

_____

If you find it difficult to experience God's love it may be due to some things in your life that need attention. Issues may come up from your past that you would rather not remember. These issues may cause you to feel shame or embarrassment. God has wiped away all your sins, and now it's time to look at some things with a different perspective. Sometimes past issues come up even though you try to push them away or try to ignore them. You are constantly trying to get ahead in life and it does not seem to be working. Well, you may say, one has absolutely nothing to do with the other. It is just that the old stuff is trying to get you down and make you feel bad about yourself.

Consider this: perhaps your ex-husband or boyfriend caused you a lot of pain. You have moved on now and choose not to think about him anymore. He may have encouraged you to participate in some activity you feel very guilty about, but you did it for him. You would like to forget you ever did it, but it keeps coming up.

Instead of feeling shame, guilt, or embarrassment, look at the incident again and decide that you will not run from the truth of it any longer. Acknowledge what you did and forgive yourself. If you caused someone else pain, deal with that, if possible. Ask God to forgive you as well. Don't be afraid of your past. Instead, learn from all you have done and then take the information, which is the lesson you learned, and leave behind the condemnation. You no longer have to feel bad about yourself. By facing the truth and dealing with the situation in love you provide true closure instead of closure in the mind only. Forgiveness is now planted in your heart.

I forgive myself for

Food for Thought:

God withheld nothing from you because of His unconditional love for you. Why then will you trust more in the love of man than in the Love of God? HMMM! HE GAVE YOU HIS LOVE, MADE YOU IN HIS IMAGE, FORGAVE YOU FOR EVERYTHING AND GAVE YOU POWER, LOVE, AND A SOUND MIND SO YOU DON'T HAVE TO FEAR REJECTION, NOT BEING LOVED, OR ANYTHING.

John 3:16 (New International Version)
"For God so loved the world that he gave his one and only Son, that whoever believes in Him shall not perish but have eternal life."

2 Timothy 1:7 (King James Version)
"For God hath not given us the spirit of fear; but of power, and of love, and of a sound mind."

Conclusion

If you fall short of what you think you ought to be doing don't worry about it, just look in the mirror at yourself and say, "NAMASKAR," which means, "I behold the Divinity in you." No matter what your situation looks like, you must behold the Divinity in yourself.

Your body is an outer shell, similar to a nut, designed as a covering for the Divinity which resides inside you. The nut has a shell to enable the precious interior fruit to survive through all types of weather and adversities. In the same way, you have surrounded yourself with a shell to protect yourself, to help you survive tough situations. Your shell can be anything from drugs to work to sex to JUST PLAIN DENIAL and more. It is that protective coating you use to keep from exposing yourself.

Something good lies inside that shell, regardless of what the exterior looks like. You must behold the goodness while the shell is being cracked. The shell can put up some resistance at times because it has been put in place to do a job, therefore it may be resistant to anything trying to crack it open. If you really want to get to the "goody" inside, behold the truth within you while the false sense of protection that has worked in the past is being cracked open and the truth is being revealed. In the midst of your challenges and victories, realize you are collecting your goodies for the difficult seasons. The lessons you are learning are eternal goodies you will use throughout your life. Gather your goodies for the rough waters ahead as the squirrel gathers his nuts for the cold season. They can make the voyage a lot smoother.

Again, I remind you to get the information (your goody) from your challenges and leave the condemnation (your shell) behind.

What nuts are you gathering to realize the great goodies you carry within?

_____

_____

_____

_____

_____

_____

_____

_____

_____

_____

_____

_____

_____

_____

_____

_____

_____

_____

_____

_____

_____

It looks like the end of the voyage, but it's really the beginning.

It is so easy to find yourself in someone else's dream or on their voyage. It is so very important to define and believe in your course. Sometimes big waves will come along or other little boats will come by and seem as if they need your help. Losing yourself, you may lend a hand. In the midst, you find that more is needed than you expected. Before you know it you are in someone else's waters sailing on their course. It's okay! Recognize what has occurred, dismiss yourself from this course, and return to your own. It's okay to help, but don't lose yourself on someone else's journey.

Remember, this is your voyage. You are here to take care of yourself, and in doing this you will be better able to assist others in a healthy way. Once you step off your course other things will place a demand on your attention and you find yourself so busy taking care of others you lose sight of your own needs. Sometimes this misdirection is hard to recognize because you are not doing anything bad; it's all in the name of helping someone else. It's easy to lose yourself in someone else's dreams and ambitions and find yours on hold, not because you consciously put them there, but because you got so busy with someone else's desires that you forgot your own.

If this happens to you, take the opportunity to return to your process and acknowledge your value apart from anyone else. Prioritize things for yourself. Staying busy can occupy you and keep you from dealing with what is real. It is an excuse not to succeed. This is often hard to see because you can be so busy, working so hard, with good intentions, and yet remain unfulfilled or dissatisfied. This can be a tiring cycle.

Now is the time to ask questions.

What's making me tired?

_____

_____

_____

_____

_____

_____

_____

_____

_____

_____

_____

_____

_____

_____

_____

_____

What do I choose to do about the things that are making me tired?

What am I really working on?

Who is this voyage really all about?

_____

_____

_____

_____

_____

_____

_____

_____

_____

_____

Am I afraid to put me out there?

_____

_____

_____

_____

_____

_____

Untitled

Am I afraid of rejection?

_____

_____

_____

_____

_____

_____

_____

_____

_____

_____

_____

_____

_____

_____

_____

_____

_____

_____

_____

_____

_____

_____

_____

_____

_____

_____

What is important to me?

There may be times when you feel as though you have conquered this process and old, familiar things show up again;
things you thought had drifted away. Don't worry if they are
still there. If this happens, just return to your journey and the
beauty of who you are. Remember, you are a success and you
have a journey of your own, a course mapped out that you
must follow because this is your voyage through life.

Food for Thought:

You cannot find your completion in someone else's dreams. You become whole and complete within your own purpose. Let no one deceive you and let nothing stand in the way of your success today.

More importantly, don't you stand in the way of your success today!

Move back into the driver's seat. Become the priority in your life right now. Value yourself. Acknowledge who you are. You are love, you are beauty, you are special, you are life, and you have so much to offer. As you walk in who you are, others will be blessed because of you. Remember that you never have to lose yourself in the process. You can give a gift and still exist. Love yourself and you will never have to worry about loving someone else, it will be a natural part of you.

Jeremiah 29:11 (New International Version)

"For I know the plans that I have for you," declares the LORD, "Plans to prosper you and not to harm you, plans to give you hope and a future."

I SEE A BRIGHT FUTURE AHEAD. GO FORTH AND PRODUCE GOOD FRUIT!

When It's All Said and Done
by Haronepthia Cameron

When it's all said and done
You will know that you, my love, have won
When the old ways will no longer do
They no longer calm or get you through

When those things are no longer enough
When going back is just too tough
You know you are ready to move on
Those times and desires are gone

You know within yourself that you are worth so much more
Move into your glory and turn back no more
Lift up your eyes, allow the wind beneath your wings
To raise you above all those useless things

You, my dear, are no longer a self-hater
You dwell now with your Creator
You no longer eat with the swine
You dwell in the Kingdom, knowing, "It's Mine"

I am now a Queen among Queens or a King among Kings
In the beauty of who I am, I shall now walk in my true Being
When it's all said and done, what is there to hold on to?
That lifestyle never did fit you!

If you ever waiver in your thought of who will assist you on your continued voyage, read:

Psalm 121 (King James Version)
"I will lift up mine eyes unto the hills, from whence cometh my help.

² My help cometh from the LORD, which made heaven and earth.

³ He will not suffer thy foot to be moved: he that keepeth thee will not slumber.

⁴ Behold, he that keepeth Israel shall neither slumber nor sleep.

⁵ The LORD is thy keeper: the LORD is thy shade upon thy right hand.

⁶ The sun shall not smite thee by day, nor the moon by night.

⁷ The LORD shall preserve thee from all evil: he shall preserve thy soul.

⁸ The LORD shall preserve thy going out and thy coming in from this time forth, and even for evermore."

Always remember:
John 16:33 (Amplified Version)
'I have told you these things, so that in Me you may have [perfect] peace and confidence. In the world you have tribulation and trials and distress and frustration; but be of good cheer [take courage; be confident, certain, undaunted]! For I have overcome the world. [I have deprived it of power to harm you and have conquered it for you.]"

Repeat this journey as many times as you need to. Start at the beginning and go through it all over again. Believe me, you will learn something new about yourself each time. New Roots produce New Fruit!

About the Author

Haronepthia Cameron has been a Registered Nurse for 20 years, and currently holds a Master's degree in Christian Counseling. She is a certified Paracletos Counselor. As a result of her experiences and the lessons learned from her own childhood, she has developed a passion to help people see how the seeds planted long ago, or even recently, may hold the answers to the problems they face today. Listening and caring about people has been a part of her life as far back as she can remember.

She learned some of her greatest lessons from her dear mother, who taught Haronepthia commitment, endurance, strength, and love in the midst of chaos. Her father taught her what it's like to struggle and fight an addiction that just won't let you be the person you really want to be. Watching this and living this gave her purpose in life. As she seeks the direction of the Holy Spirit, she is committed to helping others be free from hindrances that try to keep them rooted and grounded in a life of destruction.

To learn more about the author, visit
www.voyagersolutions.net

CPSIA information can be obtained
at www.ICGtesting.com
Printed in the USA
LVOW01s1338100316

478584LV00002B/5/P